WRITE OFFERS THAT SELL

44 PSYCHOLOGICAL STRATEGIES TO CREATE A SUCCESSFUL OFFER

ROMAN KMENTA

Imprint

© 2020 Roman Kmenta, Forstnergasse 1, A-2540 Bad Vöslau - www.romankmenta.com

1st edition 12/2020
Cover design: Monika Stern / sternloscreative

Layout: VoV media
Illustration: VoV media
Editing / proofreading: VoV media
Image right: Freepik hole-from-ball 73
Publisher: VoV media - www.voice-of-value.com

The work, including its parts, is protected by copyright. Any use is not permitted without the consent of the publisher and the author. This applies to electronic or other duplication, translation, distribution, and making it available to the public via analog and digital media and channels.

The contents of this book were created with great care. However, we cannot assume any liability for the correctness, completeness, and topicality of the content. This book contains links to external third-party websites, over whose content we have no influence. Therefore, we cannot accept any liability for this external content. The respective operator or provider of the respective pages is always responsible for the content of the linked pages. At the time of publication of this book - after checking this website - there were no indications of legal violations. Should such be known at a later point in time, we will remove the links as soon as possible.

When reproducing common names, trade names, names of goods and registered brands - in the interests of easier readability - the trademarks have been omitted.

The book refers to various products, some of which can be bought on Amazon. As an Amazon partner, the author earns from qualified sales.

Contents

Contents 3
Foreword 7
Goals for written offers 10
Build value, but how? 12
   Offer strategy #1 -
   Identify customer needs 14
   Offer strategy #2 -
   Put on the customer's glasses 15
   Offer strategy #3 -
   Customer benefits instead of just product features 15
The offer presentation 17
   Offer strategy #4 -
   Present your offers personally 18
Offer structure 22
   Offer Strategy #5 -
   Define a standard template 22
   Offer Strategy #6 -
   Create and build relationships first 23
   Offer Strategy #7 -
   Describe the customer's problems 24
   Offer strategy #8 -
   Pack the customer's specific goals into your offer 26
   Offer strategy #9 -
   Not too many details in the offer 27

*Offer strategy #10 -
Offer package pricing* 28

*Offer strategy #11 -
Give price its own page* 29

*Offer Strategy #12 -
Calculate the savings* 29

*Offer Strategy #13 -
Put a price on free products* 30

*Offer Strategy #14 -
Narrow your offerings* 31

*Offer Strategy #15 -
Formulate a Call to Action (CTA)* 33

Presentation / design **35**

*Offer strategy #16 -
Get a layout designed* 35

*Offer Strategy #17 -
Choose a larger font* 37

*Offer Strategy #18 -
Use short sentences* 38

*Offer Strategy #19 -
Use bullets and lists* 39

*Offer Strategy #20 -
Create more sections* 39

*Offer Strategy #21 -
Create subheadings* 40

*Offer Strategy #22 -
Use graphics and images* 40

*Offer strategy #23 -
Use colors and a text layout with a sure instinct* 40

Personalization 42

Offer Strategy #24 -
Use the customer logo 43

Offer Strategy #25 -
Use the customer's name 43

Offer Strategy #26 –
List customer value 44

Offer Strategy #27 -
Sign in person 44

Offer Strategy #28 -
Use a Post-it Note 45

Quoting Strategy #29 -
Include quotations 45

Text and words 48

Proposition Strategy #30 -
Create value with more words 48

Proposition Strategy #31 -
Create value in fancy and powerful words 51

Offer strategy #32 -
Write in your customer's voice 53

Price psychology 56

Offer Strategy #33 -
Make a price sandwich 56

Offer strategy #34 -
Avoid plasticizers 58

Offer Strategy #35 -
Avoid negatively associated words 59

*Offer strategy #36 -
Leave out the $ signs* 60

*Offer Strategy #37 -
Make prices small* 60

*Offer strategy #38 -
Put higher-priced items in front* 62

*Offer strategy #39 -
Do not use round prices* 65

Packaging **67**

*Offer strategy #40 -
Package your offer in a valuable way* 67

Stand out **71**

*Offer strategy #41 -
Include an audio file with the offer* 72

*Offer strategy #42 -
Package your message as a video* 72

*Offer Strategy #43 -
Make your own website for your offer* 75

*Offer Strategy #44 -
Deliver "Shock and Awe" packages* 77

Last strategy **79**

Bonus tip: Follow up - ALWAYS! 79

About the Author **82**

Foreword

Many industries work with offer letters. Yours probably does too, otherwise, you wouldn't be reading this book. Writing professional offers is, however, a highly underestimated matter. Sellers pay attention to the content of an offer, especially the price, but are usually not aware of the importance of the offer itself.

Your offers are dumb sellers (although they don't always have to be dumb; please check out a couple of very exciting ideas towards the end of the book). You communicate with the customer. Your offers - if they are well made - have more and longer customer contact than you as the seller.

In many cases, the written offer is your only contact with a customer. In many industries, it is customary to ask for a written offer first and, if there is interest, it is followed by a personal conversation with the seller. For tenders, which are a special form of business, it is all the more important that your offer does an excellent sales job.

I've written around a few thousand offers myself in my professional career. From small ones in the range of a few hundred dollars to very large ones in the range of a few hundred thousand dollars. A few - during my time in the IT industry - were in the millions.

At the start of my career, I wasn't aware of the importance of the written offer. I had no idea how diverse and in-depth the topic of "offers" is.

Today, I work with both small and very large companies and help them improve their sales performance. The content of this book - working professionally with offers - is an important tool for a company's positive sales results.

It is not difficult to get significantly more out of your offers. It is not particularly time consuming, nor does it entail significantly higher costs. Turning your offers into better sellers just takes the right strategies which you will find in this book, maybe a dash of creativity, and the consistent implementation and application of the tips you read here.

These strategies are perfectly coordinated with written offers in the form of letters or emails. You will find, however, that most of the material can also be used for the presentation of offers which you may conduct to several people. Much can also be used in the context of online offers, either on sales pages or in online shops.

However you offer, I wish you every success.

Roman Kmenta

Goals for written offers

If you optimize your offers and make them better sellers, what do you want to achieve by doing that? More sales, of course. A higher conversion rate, of course. But these are general sales elements that not only have to do with the offer itself, but also depend on many other factors, such as:

- the offer content - the products and prices
- the salespeople and their skills
- your marketing and advertising
- your company's image
- and much more.

I would, therefore, recommend that you consider goals for your offers that are more closely related to, and more directly influenced by, the offer. The goals pursued with the strategies in this book are:

- Customers should feel personally addressed by your offer.
- Customers should keep your offer for as long as possible (and not just throw it away quickly).

- Your offer should stand out positively from the offers of the competition and attract attention.
- Your offer should enhance what you provide.
- Your offer should communicate to the customer that you are a very professional supplier.

And yes, even if it is not the immediate goal of the offer, the strategies and tips in this book should, and will, contribute a great deal to that, bringing:

- increased rates of conversion
- your offers accepted more often
- growth in sales
- higher price scales and more income generated.

Build value, but how?

How much is something worth? That question cannot be answered universally. The value arises in the mind of the customer; it's a very individual, subjective matter.

Some people go heavily into debt for the latest big-screen TV; others don't even own a TV. Some companies reside in luxurious offices at fancy addresses, others work out of containers. It is not necessarily about being able to afford something; often those who work in containers are the more profitable.

Rather, it is about what, or under what circumstances, someone is willing to spend (more) money. And that is exactly what is determined by the value that is attached to a certain product or service.

This value can be increased by you as the seller, and by your offers. Essentially, all of the strategies listed below are concerning how you can increase the value of your offer.

Customer benefit as the basis

The basis of all sales considerations is the customer benefit, or the purchase motives on which the customer benefit is based. Buying motives are based on human needs. If we ignore the basic needs (food, air, etc.), there are a number of needs or buying motives that control your customers' purchasing decisions.

Some possible reasons for buying include:

- Prestige and recognition
- Connection with others/love
- Growth and progress
- Saving costs
- Making a profit
- Security and control
- Freedom
- Power
- Variety
- Simplicity and freedom from problems
- Health
- Enjoyment
- Helping others and contributing to the whole.

To increase the individual value of your offer in the customer's mind it is necessary to address the appropriate or decisive purchase motive of the customer. Only then does what you do add value.

Simply put, if a customer has a very high need for safety, then emphasizing the fact that a vehicle type has never been involved in a fatal accident falls on fertile ground. However, if it is crucial to the customer to drive as cheaply as possible and save costs, this argument is less powerful.

This means that you should know the individual needs of your customers as precisely as possible to then tailor your offer, and any other form of customer communication, to them in the best possible way.

Offer strategy #1 - Identify customer needs

You can discover what a customer's needs are by applying a thorough needs analysis in the customer meeting. This is the foundation for successful selling. Among other things, the question, "What is particularly important to you if you ..." is perfect for this. The customer is very likely to first answer the points that are most important to them and that correspond to their most critical needs.

And when you get the customer to talk, make notes about the key points.

Offer strategy #2 -
Put on the customer's glasses

Always remember the preparation of an offer is not about your products and services, and certainly not about you (as hard as that sounds), but exclusively about your customers, their needs, and their benefits. The risk is high that a seller will write best about what he likes or what would be a motive for him to buy.

> *The bait has to taste good*
> *to the fish, not to the angler.*

So, keep asking yourself, "What does it do for my customer?" And write exactly that in your offer letter.

Offer strategy #3 -
Customer benefits instead of just product features

Especially in the case of technical products and where products have a variety of characteristics, sellers tend to cram offers with all these characteristics. MB, MzH, horsepower, number of airbags, speed, wall thickness, insulation values - there are countless product features depending on what you are selling.

Product features must be included in an offer, but a feature is not a motive to buy. You should, therefore, translate the most important product features into customer benefits.

- After the thermal renovation, the energy efficiency of your house will improve from class F to class B. This can you save approx. $7 per year in energy costs per m^2 of living space. Calculated for your entire house, you will save around $ 1,500 per year.

You could formulate advantages in your offers similar to the above.

Starting points for increasing value

Once motivation to buy has been clarified, a number of other areas offer a great deal of potential to increase the value of your offer in the eyes of the customers.

These areas, that we will cover in the course of this book, are:
- the offer presentation
- the structure of the offer
- the offer design
- the words and texts used
- pricing and price psychology
- the packaging of your offer
- stand out and special forms of offers .

The offer presentation

When presenting the offer, the question is, "How does the customer receive your offer?" The question sounds a bit banal, especially since nowadays offers are mostly sent by email. But there are many more possibilities behind it than you would first think.

The method of receipt only becomes significant later in the process, but I mention it now because the way you present your offer to the customer will have an impact on the other subjects we cover in this book.

Graded according to their effectiveness, you have essentially five options for presenting your offers to customers:

1. Personally by a presentation
2. Via Skype or similar online tool
3. By phone in combination with email
4. By post
5. By email

Offer strategy #4 -
Present your offers personally

Whenever there is time and the size of the potential order demands it, you should present your offers personally instead of just sending them.

This has several advantages as follows:

- The offer letter is no longer silent; you can explain your offer.
- You can present it nicely printed out and packaged in a suitable folder, which, of course, has to fit your business, and thus enhance it.
- You will notice how your customer reacts to your offer. Does he fall off his chair at the price, or does he breathe a sigh of relief?
- You can answer questions or resolve objections immediately.
- You can close the deal directly if necessary; that doesn't work if you write your offer and send it by post or email.
- The probability of receiving the order increases, because with your personal visit and by presenting your letter of offer face-to-face you show how important the customer is to you.

Ideally, you should not send the offer to your customer in advance, because if he sees it before you present it to him in person, you lose some of the advantages mentioned above.

The bigger the business or the higher the price and the more significant the customer, the more vital a personal presentation of your offer is. But even if you do not yet know the customer well, you should seek personal contact when presenting an offer of magnitude.

Other alternatives to the offer presentation

As mentioned above, there are other ways in which you can present your offer or send it to the customer, as below.

Via Skype

A video conference via Skype or similar online tool is the closest thing to a face-to-face meeting, so this is the second-best option. You can still see and hear the customer's reaction. The presentation of the offer page-by-page or split into sections is also very possible.

This is an exciting option, especially when customers are further away. Interestingly, however, it is not used very much.

By phone

If an online connection is not possible or desired, you can present your offer by phone and thus partly be able to gauge your customer's reactions. You can email the offer itself at the same time. All in all, it is not as elegant as online, but possible.

By post

The now little used variant of sending the offer by post has some advantages. You can make the offer as valuable as you want (nice paper, folder, etc. - more on this later), and if your offer is then next to competitors' pitches that were sent by email and simply printed out, you are very likely to attract positive attention.

I often hear that people don't choose the postal service because customers need offers quickly. At the same time, there are very few industries in which a day or two by post is really significant.

By email

The last and most unattractive variant of the offer presentation is to send your offers by email. I would only recommend this if the previous variants cannot be used for whatever reasons.

Some customers want to have the offers digitally anyway, so they can forward them more easily internally or store them digitally. If that is the case, you can always submit it in digital form in addition to the other variant you have chosen.

Offer structure

Now that we have decided which way to deliver the offer presentation, let's go back to the start. This is about the structure of your offers.

The basis of your written offer should be a logical and easily understandable offer structure that covers all potential points and questions that your customer will have in mind. It is the framework for a written offer.

Offer Strategy #5 - Define a standard template

You do not need to reinvent the structure for each of your offers. Define a style that you can use again and again. This template not only provides the structure, but also includes a number of the other points that we will come to in this book. This saves you a lot of time when preparing your written offers.

The psychologically correct structure of the offer

The structure of your written offers and the order in which you present your content is based on the structure of a good, professional sales pitch. Your offer is a silent seller, so it should behave like one.

Offer Strategy #6 - Create and build relationships first

One of the biggest mistakes that one finds again and again with bad offers, and that bad sellers also make, is simply to list the service components and give them a price. At the beginning and the end are just short, meaningless phrases.

That may be enough for a very short, highly standardized offer that involves low amounts. It is definitely not enough for more complex and, above all, higher value offers.

As in a real sales pitch, you need to create and build relationships with the offer first. You do that with the below structure.

Structure of a written offer

Below, you will find the essential parts of an offer that is supposed to sell in the correct order from a psychological perspective. In addition, your offer must contain other components depending on the industry and service.

On the one hand, these can be legal-formal things such as cancellation deadlines or expense regulations. On the other hand, it may also be necessary to add very product, or company, specific information in the appropriate places.

1. Initial situation

Describe briefly (in two to three sentences) the initial situation in which your customer finds themselves. If possible, address the customer's problems. By increasing their awareness of the problem, the chances that your offer will be accepted as the solution to their problems increases.

Offer Strategy #7 - Describe the customer's problems

Some examples:

- **Sales training:**
  The sales force conducts 10-15 sales calls per day. There is a wide range of fluctuations in deals between 20% for the weakest sellers and 50% for the best. Due to this underperformance of some sellers, the company loses sales of around $350,000 per month.

- **Windows:**
  The house will get new windows as part of a comprehensive thermal renovation. The old,

partially leaky windows result in additional heating costs amounting to a few hundred euros per year.

- **Advertising campaign:**
  The new model XY with the innovative Z technology will be launched in early December. The launch of the model had to be postponed twice. This creates a high, short-term pressure to succeed.

It could be something like that. You only need to include the information that the customer has given you as part of the needs analysis and include it in your offer - if possible even in the customer's words.

It is not about conveying new information to the customer, but only about picking up the first yes. The customer should think, "He has listened to me and understood me."

2. Goals

In the next step you formulate the goals that the customer is pursuing in his project. What does he want to achieve? You also received this information in the needs analysis.

Offer strategy #8 - Pack the customer's specific goals into your offer

Some examples:

- **Sales training:**
  The goal that you are pursuing with this measure is to increase the completion rate by 20% and thus increase your sales to an average of $1,000 per salesperson per day.

- **Windows:**
  The installation of the new windows should save an additional $300 in heating costs per year.

- **Advertising campaign:**
  By means of the planned campaign, the awareness of the new model in the target group should be 50% within two months.

Formulate these goals as specifically as possible and, above all, orientate them towards customer benefit as described above.

3. Concept

Now is the time to present your concept, which is the solution to the customer's problems and with which they can, and will, achieve their goals. You can do this - depending on what you offer - in two steps:

- Overview of the concept
- List specific service components with individual customer benefits.

Offer strategy #9 -
Not too many details in the offer

Be as detailed as necessary, but no more. Your offer should not be a cemetery of numbers and data. A solution that is suitable for offers with a lot of detailed information is to give an overview with the most important details in the offer itself. All further information - for those who want it – are enclosed in a separate document.

4. Prices

When it comes to the prices for your service or your products, there are a few things to consider and a few questions to be answered.

Package prices or individual prices

Do you quote an individual price for each specific service component in your offer, or not? The answer to this question also has to do with the nature of your partial services.

- For parts of the service that can be sold individually, please quote detailed prices.

- If only the entire package can be purchased, do not state the detailed prices.

- If you want to highlight individual, particularly favorable, detailed prices, list them.

- If you want to avoid the prices of parts of your offer being discussed separately, do not list them.

Offer strategy #10 - Offer package pricing

I am an advocate of offering package pricing wherever it makes sense. Package prices have the following advantages:

- Your offer is more difficult to compare with that of the competition. It is generally good to avoid comparability, especially if your offer – when compared 1:1 - is not the cheapest.

- You find it easier to sell more. It only takes a single YES to sell a package. For the basic model plus various additional equipment, the customer has to say YES several times.

Offer strategy #11 - Give price its own page

Especially if you intend to present your offer personally to the customer, you should sacrifice a whole sheet and give the price, above all the final price, its own page. Why?

When you sit with the customer and go through the offer together with them, and while you are still explaining the service components, if the price is already visible at the bottom of the same page where will the customer's attention be focused?

Right, on the price! Instead, think about the benefits you are explaining. If you send the offer by mail, this effect is not so important as you have no control over how your customer reads the offer. At the same time, it doesn't hurt to always separate the price.

Offer Strategy #12 - Calculate the savings

If there are any kind of savings for the customer as part of your offer, like a discount, a bonus, a credit, a special price, etc. - then you should definitely highlight these savings.

The following rules apply:

- for small amounts (less than $100) as a percentage
    - You save 20%.
- for larger amounts, in absolute numbers
    - You save $350.

Why? The psychology is simple. With a $10 product, a $2 saving does not sound as much as 20%. With a $250,000 project, 2% doesn't sound like a lot, but $5,000 is a lot of money.

Offer Strategy #13 -
Put a price on free products

If you give something away for free as part of the offer, you should still put a price on it.

What costs nothing is worth nothing.

Even if you never sell this free product and always give it away, it must have a price. With a price, you create value for the free product and thus upgrade your offer.

5. Benefit

Immediately after the prices, summarize the main benefit or benefits for the customer in your offer.

Example:

- **Sales training:**
  With this offer, you can be sure that you have taken important steps to significantly increase the closing rates of your sales team. The basis for the sales growth you are aiming for is laid down.

6. Offer validity

The validity of the offer is, of course, something that must be stated on most offers for legal and formal reasons. There could be changes in costs, which then lead to higher prices. Therefore, the provider must maintain a certain flexibility and must not be tied to his offer forever.

But going beyond this simple purpose, the validity of the offer also has a sales psychological background. This has to do with a psychological lever - scarcity. This states that things that are scarcer or rarer, things that not everyone can always have, become more valuable.

Offer Strategy #14 - Narrow your offerings

This apparent shortage can be achieved in different ways. Apart from the cases where the product is genuinely in short supply, something of which there is only a certain amount, maybe even only one piece, one can artificially shorten products and services.

This strategy is often used in sales and marketing. Many, including many customers, know and understand the intent behind it. Interestingly, however, this does not mean that the shortage does not create its psychological effect anyway, as I can recognize time and again in myself. Many behavioral, psychological studies have also proven this outcome and its effectiveness again and again.

You can use this shortage in two main ways when the offer is valid:

- shortage of quantities
    - Only three of these are available.
    - Only while stocks last.
- shortage of time
    - The offer is only valid until ....

The shortage puts a certain amount of pressure on the customer who is interested in your offer. It leads to a quicker decision on what is on offer - especially when there is a shortage of quantities.

When there is a shortage of time, it has been shown time and again that many customers buy just before the offer expires.

7. Next steps

At the end of your offer, you should tell the customer what, from your point of view, the next steps are. It seems clear to many sellers that the customer should, of course, buy. Does that really have to be said or written separately? Yes, absolutely.

It has been shown that the indolence of human choice requires us to be told exactly what to do. In technical jargon, one speaks of a "Call to Action (CTA)". It's always amazing how much a CTA affects order rates.

In the case of online offers, much has been and is being worked with CTAs and many tests and comparisons are carried out, which are very simple to do and can be precisely evaluated in online purchase processes. In addition to many other elements and features, such as color, positioning, and size of the buy buttons, the formulation of the CTA has a significant effect on success.

Offer Strategy #15 - Formulate a Call to Action (CTA)

The rule is to be as striking and direct as possible, for example "Click here now." If you translate this knowledge to a physical, written offer in the form of a letter or presentation (which does not have any purchase buttons), this means that you finally tell the customer what you expect from them now.

After all, a human salesperson should do that in a sales pitch. As mentioned, an effective offer corresponds in many ways to a professional and successful sales pitch.

Examples of calls to action:

- Get the benefits from this offer today and call me at XYZ (it's not a bad idea to be a little gentle on time here, too).

- We look forward to carrying out this project with you. If you share this view, then sign this offer and send it back to us.

- Secure your place and confirm this offer right away (shortage of quantity is an effective lever in sales psychology).

Presentation / design

The structure of your offer, which we have discussed above, is the foundation of everything else. The presentation is primarily about the visual implementation within the structure.

The main aim of the following strategies and tips is to make your offer easier to read and understand. People's attention spans have become significantly shorter in recent years. We have forgotten how to concentrate on reading longer texts; no wonder, since we practice the art of shortened communication on social media for many hours a day.

Your offer should therefore follow this trend and consist of short, easily comprehensible information units.

Offer strategy #16 -
Get a layout designed

Before we go into details, however, one important point in advance. Most offers are relatively carelessly written in Word or, even worse, are the result of calculation software, especially in the technical area.

I often hear from customers who work with this type of software that what I say is correct but cannot be implemented in their software. I do not understand this approach. Software should help you to make better offers, but in no way limit your design.

The problem is that this type of software was mostly created by technicians and programmers and not by salespeople or people with an understanding of marketing and sales psychology, let alone graphical instinct.

Accordingly, these standard templates are often terrible.

Since you want to, and should, use your template often, you can invest a little creativity and money here. If you are not one yourself, I would recommend hiring a graphic designer who will work with you to develop an optimal layout for your offers.

Layout elements:

- Format: landscape, portrait, square etc.
- Fonts (style and legibility) for running texts and headings
- Font sizes
- Colors
- Frame
- Backgrounds

- Standard graphics and images.

The aim is that your template:

- looks valuable
- fits your industry and your products
- suits your customers
- is flexibly adaptable
- is easy to process and fill.

Offer Strategy #17 - Choose a larger font

For your offers, especially for those parts that are to be read, choose a slightly larger font than is usual or necessary. This makes the offer a little longer, but that is not a problem.

Especially if your customers are no longer very young, the font size is decisive for how easily or how enthusiastically your offer is read. I notice in myself that I avoid reading texts that are too small, also because I still refuse to wear reading glasses.

How big is big enough? It depends on which format you are using. For offers in Powerpoint, landscape format (similar to a presentation) I use a font size of 16 points for the body text, and 18 - 20 points for headings. That would be too small for a proper presentation in front of several customers.

For offers in Word, letter format, 16 points are too large. Here I would use at least 12 points, maybe even 14 points.

Offer Strategy #18 - Use short sentences

As mentioned, we are all used to reading short sentences. The longer the sentences, the more difficult the offer is to read and understand.

So, write your offer first without thinking about the length of the sentences. In a revision pass, check the length of your sentences and shorten them. In the simplest case, you can turn a longer one into two short sentences.

Sentence length is an important criterion for the comprehensibility of a text, but by no means the only thing. Some experts deal scientifically with the subject of measuring the intelligibility of a text. You don't have to go that far. Shorter sentences are a very good basis.

However, if you want to go into the subject in greater depth without a lot of effort, there are online tools, some of which are free, in which you can enter your text and which analyze them in detail with regard to their comprehensibility according to various criteria.

Two examples for such tools can be found here:

- https://readabilityformulas.com/freetests/six-readability-formulas.php

- https://www.webfx.com/tools/readable/check.php

Offer Strategy #19 - Use bullets and lists

Bullet points and lists will greatly improve the readability of your offers. Instead of packing the information into running text, which is partially okay, list them as bullets or in list form.

You can support this with graphic elements by adding to the list e.g. B. pack in a table with a frame.

Offer Strategy #20 - Create more sections

Many offer texts suffer from overlong paragraphs. Get into the habit of making shorter paragraphs. After two, or a maximum of three sentences, or lines, create another paragraph. This makes legibility much easier.

Offer Strategy #21 - Create subheadings

If you make more paragraphs, you can increase the effect by adding one or more subheadings.

Offer Strategy #22 - Use graphics and images

"A picture is worth a thousand words!" This old wisdom still has meaning, even when it comes to your offers. Images and graphics can work wonders, especially with very technical products and services that require more detailed explanation.

Offer strategy #23 - Use colors and a text layout with a sure instinct

As much as colors, different fonts, underlining, bold text etc. can improve the legibility and impact of your offer, it can also be overdone. Too much of it quickly becomes cheesy, cheap, and devaluing.

You should, therefore, also define your standard layout with a graphic designer how much to include, and what is OK and what is not.

In principle, all of these options for designing your offers are easy to use but are often not used. If you follow these guidelines, however, your offer will be visually different from the offers of the competitors and appear much more professional, and also more personable.

Personalization

We live in a time when customers want everything to be very personal. There are very few products uninfluenced by this trend towards personalization. You can even put together your car - a product that used to be highly standardized - and configure it online to suit your taste. The trend is called mass customization.

So, it is only logical that your offers should also leave the customer with the impression that you have made this offer especially for them. And with a few tricks and strategies, this can be done easily and quickly. You don't have to reinvent the offer every time.

More precisely, personalization has two aspects:

- Tailoring the offer to the customer as much as possible - not only in terms of content, but also formally.
- Expressing that you personally put a lot of effort into writing this offer for the customer.

Offer Strategy #24 - Use the customer logo

To start with something simple, use the customer's logo in your listing if you have companies as clients, simply because that is something that I see already implemented in many offers. But, be careful. To be on the safe side, research exactly which logo is the current one. Logos change and using an old logo (as has happened to me before) is embarrassing.

Offer Strategy #25 - Use the customer's name

What do people prefer to hear or read? Their own name! And second best? Their own name! And third favorite? Right, you've got the hang of it, their own name!

That may seem exaggerated, but I have seen studies that back it up. And you can test it yourself, even without studies. How do you feel when you arrive somewhere where you are a regular and are greeted by name? Feels good, doesn't it?

And now, imagine going into a store where you seldom go, e.g. three times a year, and are greeted there by name (that happened to me at a shoemaker's and I don't know exactly how he did it). Fantastic, but almost spooky in times of data protection regulations.

Incorporate the name of the customer (the person), or the name of the company if you are in the B2B area, from time to time in your offers. Certainly in the cover letter if you are using a separate one, but also in the offer itself, where it fits.

Offer Strategy #26 – List customer value

At the risk of repeating myself—we already dealt with this at the beginning of the book—it's imperative that you incorporate the most significant customer benefit(s) into your offer.

Work through your offer again and check whether you have included it, or where you can further express the customer benefit in the offer.

Offer Strategy #27 - Sign in person

A manual signature also gives your offer a personal touch. Ideally - if you print out the offer and send it by paper post it must include a real signature from you.

If you want to go one better and make your signature even more valuable, then sign with a fountain pen. It has more style and looks even more personal. You might even use a fountain pen with a slightly wider tip; that looks really good. And preferably in a dark blue or green ink; this will also make you stand out.

If you send the offer electronically, then scan your signature. Use a different color for this; blue or green for example. This makes the signature look a little more real. Black signatures look like they have been copied.

By the way, if you get someone to sign the letter for you, you are saying nothing more than, *"Dear customer, you are not important enough to me, so I have had a subordinate sign this document so I have more time to devote myself to really important people."*

Offer Strategy #28 - Use a Post-it Note

If you want to add another personal touch to your offer, use Post-it Notes or similar tools for marking. With all the professionalism you should strive for in your offer, you make it more human and thus more personable if you specifically mark a place, for example use a Post-it Note with an arrow or a note on it, or leave a personal note.

Quoting Strategy #29 - Include quotations

This is a supply strategy that may not fit every scenario, but it can be used well. At the same time, you can use quotations to underline and highlight arguments, product features, customer benefits and, in general, statements that are important to you. Quotes are an effective way to emotionalize your offers.

Quotations can, for example, be used in such a way that they fit the respective section of the offer. So, I use quotes myself in the standard template of my offers.

Examples of this from my offers for further training measures in companies are:

- **Aims**
  "Success is not measured by goals, but by continuous improvement." – Tiger Woods

- **Concept and implementation**
  "Success is the result of good preparation, hard work, and learning from failure!" – Colin Powell

- **Price part**
  "An investment in knowledge always brings the highest returns." - Benjamin Franklin

Emotions make the difference and add value

As mentioned above, providers in technical industries tend to limit their written offers to numbers, data, and facts. When you write your offers in this way, you literally urge your customers to focus on the price as the only differentiating factor, implying comparable quality and quantity with the competition. And that only makes sense if you are the cheapest.

With many of the strategies already discussed (customer benefits, images, quotes, etc.) and some of those that we will discuss, you will also bring more emotionality to your offer. Use everything possible to make your offers more emotional. This not only sets you apart from other providers, but also enhances your offer at the same time.

Text and words

The words you use when writing offers greatly affects your customer's perception of value. It is about the right words, words that are suitable for creating more numerous, nicer, and larger images in the minds of your customers. At the same time, the number of words used makes a difference in value perception.

Proposition Strategy #30 - Create value with more words

First, this strategy is not just about producing a lot of text. That would just result in an illegible mess of letters that would be off-putting.

Rather, replicate the strategy of top restaurateurs in your offers. What do they do? They are masters at making their food and drinks appear much more valuable with the right words.

I live in Bad Vöslau, a wine-growing area south of Vienna. The winegrowers are not only wine producers, but also innkeepers (so-called "Heurige") who open their doors every few weeks for almost two weeks.

You can eat and drink wine there, in a nice, down-to-earth atmosphere and at very reasonable prices. The *schnitzel*—made from pork or chicken—costs $7-9 and is, mostly, large and tastes very good.

But what if you ordered the same pork schnitzel in an upscale restaurant. How much would that cost? $20, $25 or even more?

It would seem very strange to us if the menu in a two or three-star restaurant simply said "pork schnitzel." We wouldn't be willing to spend $25 on that, would we? The restaurateur has to work a little harder and tap his/her literary streak.

"Juicy Wiener Schnitzel from our organic, young Styrian pigs raised on fresh clover and humanely prepared," or something like that could be the description. Let that sink in and decide for yourself. Has this increased the value of the schnitzel?

Words create value.

Of course, an eloquent description of food is not the only lever used by top gastronomy venues, but it is a significant one. And one that can be used in all industries.

Here are few examples of this:

An industrial company could use a material named:

- Plastic
- Special plastic
- Abrasion-resistant, special plastic
- Abrasion-resistant, high-tech plastic
- Extremely abrasion-resistant, high-tech plastic
- Extremely abrasion-resistant, high-tech plastic from space research.

Or a service provider who gives lectures and keynotes, like me, could name them:

- A presentation
- An inspiring talk
- An extremely inspiring lecture
- An enormously inspiring and pointed lecture
- An enormously inspiring and remarkably pointed lecture
- An enormously inspiring, remarkably pointed, and humorous presentation
- An enormously inspiring, remarkably pointed, and extremely humorous presentation.

You decide how big the difference is in the effect. How much more valuable your offer is in the mind of your customer through the targeted use of this strategy we will probably not find out exactly, as we cannot look into his head. However, common sense suggests that this increases the value.

Proposition Strategy #31 - Create value in fancy and powerful words

The second part of the "word strategy" is to use nicer, fancier, and more powerful words than your competitors. Words that create bigger, more engaging images in your customers' minds.

A branded company would hardly bring a new product onto the market and advertise it as a "very good new model."

Adjectives - THE weapon to increase the value

Adjectives, in particular, are especially good at increasing value. For example, what can we think of to use instead of *"good"*?

> *extraordinary, outstanding, successful, excellent, optimal, effective, useful, to the point, ideal, special, extraordinary, impressive, significant, stunning, fabulous, fantastic, enchanting, delightful, brilliant, grandiose, extraordinary, efficient, excellent, great, brilliant, fantastic, world class, supernatural, radiant, gigantic, extraterrestrial, mythical, divine, (inter-)*

galactic, the burner, cool, phenomenal, electrifying, tasty, delicate, tingling, crisp, pointed, smart, sexy, clever, high-quality, precise, inspiring, hot, remarkable, wonderful, sensational, great, noble, enviable, worthy of imitation, brilliant, insane, admirable, awesome, awe-inspiring, adorable, unbelievable, otherworldly, erotic, epochal, magical, once in a lifetime, an eleven on a ten-point scale ... just to name a few examples.

And then, there are all the combinations (often with *real, extra, special, extraordinary* etc.) such as *"extraordinarily admirable," "incredibly ingenious,"* or *"really remarkable."*

A friend of mine prefers to use a negatively associated noun to express his greatest admiration and says something like, *"The food was really a killer!"* which goes to show that there are only a few limits to the imagination.

Word magic: Adding value by generating emotions

But why this "gimmick" with words? Quite simply, the semantic response; the influence that a word has on a person's thoughts and emotions is totally different between *"good"* and *"extremely adorable."*

Offer strategy #32 -
Write in your customer's voice

There is one more crucial aspect of your offerings related to the words you use. Earlier in the book, we have discussed in detail that it is vital that you clearly express the customer benefit in your offers.

But that is not enough, or rather, you can intensify the effect. Imagine handing over a package to your customer. The contents of the package are what the customer wants. But, as you may know from your own experience with gifts, the packaging of the package is extremely significant, it is sometimes even more important than the contents.

In the case of sales communication in general, words are used to package the contents of your offer. And the customer prefers to hear words they use themselves. This is related to the fact that we generally like what is similar to us.

If you paid close attention and wrote diligently in your briefing or your needs assessment in preparation for drafting the offer, then you have a collection of customer-specific words and—sometimes industry-specific—expressions that you can then use when writing offers.

When you formulate the offer text, incorporate these with as much familiarity as possible, just as the customer uses them. Subconsciously, your customer will feel much better understood by you when they find their own words in the offer letter.

What words do your customers use?

- Sensational.
- Sustainability.
- Effectiveness.

There are thousands of other examples. The more eccentric your customer's expressions, the more productive this strategy is when writing an offer. Often, words and entire metaphors from your customer's hobbies are reflected in their language.

- The new product is a hole-in-one.
- *"I would like my employees to get a better grip on the goal."* One of my customers once said to communicate to me that they would like their salespeople to be more goal-oriented and closer to the target.

Enter the customer's world; it is a real gold treasure for your offer.

For example, a friend of mine uses the word "sensational" conspicuously often and very happily. This is a word that

I, myself, rarely use. But if I wanted to recommend a restaurant to this friend, the recommendation would be most effective if I made it palatable to him with the words, *"I was in a really sensational restaurant yesterday."*

Price psychology

Price psychology also offers fruitful possibilities when it comes to making your offers more valuable or making the prices you quote appear smaller than they actually are. And if the price is less than the value, the customer will choose your offer.

Offer Strategy #33 - Make a price sandwich

This pricing-related strategy is about preventing the customer from thinking about price. This is especially important if you are not the cheapest provider (which will be the case for the vast majority of readers, since there can only be one cheapest).

Of course, we can't completely stop the customer from thinking about the price. They'll definitely do that. Still, we should do our best to get them to focus on **value** rather than price.

Make sure the price isn't the very last thing in your offer letter. The price must be followed by customer benefits.

This increases the chance that your customer will be concerned with the benefit rather than the price.

Wrap your price in a so-called "price sandwich," which—like a classic sandwich—has three layers.

An example of a fully formulated option:

1. **Offer feature**
   This two-day sales training for your field staff will focus on the subject of price negotiations, including the customization concept and a follow-up webinar, ...

2. **Prize**
   for $6,900 and ...

3. **Benefit**
   ...have thus created a solid basis for increasing your margins and contribution by the targeted 10% and earning significantly more.

If you have already listed your characteristics and the prices for them, then add one or two sentences with benefit formulations after the list.

Offer strategy #34 - Avoid plasticizers

Softeners are words and expressions that weaken what we say and reduce the strength of the message. Especially when it comes to prices, it is important that they are communicated powerfully and with a lot of self-confidence.

When analyzing a customer's offers, I used the following standard formulation after the price was mentioned:

- We hope our prices correspond with your expectations.

What does that mean for the customer? If they don't, is there a better, lower price? This is a classic example of a plasticizer.

More often than full sentences, individual words act as softeners and dramatically reduce the chance of getting your prices through. Such attenuating words are found much more often in the spoken language than in the written language (luckily for your offers), but you should still keep a critical eye on your offer formulation.

Common examples are:

- could, would, should, might
- actually, normally, if appropriate, possibly

It is incredibly easy for us to slip these into price quotations when we speak.

The list price can also be understood as a plasticizer. *"The list price for this is ..."* also implies that there is another, lower price than this that could be used. In this case, simply leave out the word *"list."* *"The price for this is ..."* is much more solid.

All in all, plasticizers can cost you a lot of money. A wrong word in the right place in the offer is often worth a large amount.

Offer Strategy #35 -
Avoid negatively associated words

A little tip that goes with the previous one is to replace words like "costs" or "pay" with other, more appropriate ones. What do I mean by that?

"Costs" are something nobody likes to have, either professionally or privately. The word automatically arouses negative associations, and you certainly do not want to awaken those in connection with your offers.

We don't like to "pay" either. *"You will pay me for that!"* Or *"You will still pay for that!"* Does not fill one with pleasant images either.

So get used to not referring to your prices in offers as "costs," but rather as an "investment." Admittedly, "investment" would look or sound very strange at the cheese counter in the supermarket. Conversely, in the case of products or services that are large and valuable, enough to be used in a written offer, the word "investment" can almost always be used.

Offer strategy #36 - Leave out the $ signs

This is another small, simple strategy that is used again and again in the catering industry. Studies suggest that customers are a little more willing to spend when the currency symbol is not next to the price.

So just write the number without the $ symbol as the price in your offer. At the appropriate point below, write something like, "All prices in $ VAT excl." This satisfies the legal formalities and the price psychology as well.

Offer Strategy #37 - Make prices small

If it fits your offer, break the prices down to suitable, smaller units and show these instead of larger bundles, depending, of course, on what is sensible or legally possible in the individual case.

A classic example here is when car dealers price the leasing rates per month or even per day in their offers. This makes the prices look lower. From a psychological point of view, this lowers the hurdle.

To which units can you break down the prices in your offers? To days, hours, minutes, people, kilometers, meters, applications, kilograms, grams, or pieces? Sometimes, it is precisely unusual approaches in your industry that can be exciting for this purpose. Make use of this price psychology effect when you write an offer.

Practical examples:

- Calculate the price of a car per day, which is often done with leasing, or per mile or kilometer.
- Calculate the prices of windows and doors based on the product life cycle and break them down to months or years.
- Calculate real estate prices down to the number of years of use or months, taking into account that the house or apartment still has value in the end.
- Calculate the investment for company seminars per participant instead of per day or, in the case of a longer training program, break down the participant prices to a per month value.

Offer strategy #38 -
Put higher-priced items in front

The order in which the products or services are listed also has an impact on the customer's decision and the outcome. The so-called anchor effect is well known in psychology. Among other things, this plays a major role in prices, as a price anchor.

Ultimately, a customer can only determine whether a price is high or low by making a comparison. We make these comparisons automatically whenever we are interested in a product and see the price of it.

We compare with previous purchases of the same or similar products, with prices of competitor products, or with the price that we previously imagined or expected. Ultimately, we compare with the value we attach to an offer in our head.

On the basis of this comparison, we then assess whether something is expensive or cheap or whether it corresponds exactly to our value proposition.

High prices for comparison

We have been working in this whole book, as mentioned at the beginning, to increase the perceived value of your offer to influence this comparison in your favor. You can also use the price anchor by giving the customer a high price as a comparison value.

You then put this high price—the most expensive variant of your offer—at the front. The customer should see that first. Perhaps that is too expensive for him and it would never be an option for him to opt for this variant, but that's not so important. The real purpose of this high-priced variant is to use the anchor effect and to make the price of the other variants that you offer appear cheaper, which is what they are compared with the most expensive variant.

Create luxury variants

In some industries, it can even make sense to create your own, particularly high-priced product variants, precisely for this purpose. Admittedly, this is easier with services than with products. With the latter, however, you can also work with packages and thus calculate a higher total price.

As mentioned, the point is not to sell this luxury variant as often as possible; the main purpose is to make the next, cheaper product appear significantly less pricey and thus sell it more often.

If you do not want to, or cannot, suggest different variants in your offer, then you can still use this strategy. Just put those parts of your offer in front that have a comparatively higher price (which does not mean that they have to be expensive).

List prices as a price anchor

Some companies and industries work with list prices that are well above the prices actually offered and achieved, hence often also called "moon prices".

Every customer also knows that these will never be achieved. Nevertheless, it makes sense to use them as a price anchor and cite them as a psychological comparison value.

Priming - an amazing phenomenon

If that is also not possible in your case, then price psychology has another, astonishing, fact to deliver. This anchor effect also unfolds its effect if the high numbers are not prices at all, but some other number. This psychological effect is also known as priming—the often unconscious influencing of the processing of a stimulus—in our case, the price.

Examples of numbers that have nothing to do with price:

- The service life for XY is 10,000 operating hours.
- 10,000,000 customers are already enjoying this product.

- An estimated 100,000,000 people worldwide have exactly this problem.

Interestingly, this correct order strategy is often not used. In fact, the opposite is seen much more often, when a list starts with the lowest prices. For example, drinks menus have the cheapest wines at the beginning and the good wines at the end. It's a shame, because, conversely, restaurateurs would make more sales and customers would enjoy better wine if they were listed the other way around.

Offer strategy #39 - Do not use round prices

How do these two price options for a condo sound to you?

- $ 350,000
- $ 351,350

How do they differ in their effect? In which case would you likely get a better price?

Real estate is a product area in which there is a lot of negotiation. Hardly any apartment or house is sold at the price offered. On the one hand, of course, this has to do with the fact that a lot of money is involved and therefore a lot can be saved. At the same time, negotiating in the real estate sector also has a tradition.

The following effect has been found in property prices. If an offer was made on non-round prices ($351,350 in our example), negotiations were also carried out, but the price achieved was ultimately higher than with round prices ($350,000). Why?

Prices that are too round are often valued and read like an invitation to negotiate. "At $351,350, the seller must have thought of something," the potential buyer automatically thinks. Out of round prices are calculated precisely. At the same time, it is assumed that there is less room for negotiation when prices are calculated so precisely.

Therefore, show non-round prices in your offers. In some industries, these arise automatically anyway, because the prices are traditionally calculated based on an exact cost calculation of many components, for example, this is often the case in the craft sector. In other areas, you simply make the prices in your offer not round.

Packaging

Not only the verbal packaging of your offer, or the increase in value through the appropriate layout, are important in influencing the value and thus the achievable price. The physical packaging also has a strong effect and can be a key success factor for your offers.

Offer strategy #40 - Package your offer in a valuable way

Some factors and elements with which you can work here have already been mentioned in the book. Here you will find another compact summary of what you should pay attention to in the physical presentation and design of your offer.

It should be noted that all of this must always be seen with consideration for the image that you embody of your products and your customers. For very down-to-earth target customers, overly luxurious offer packaging can be a shot that backfires. With a little sensitivity, however, you can collect decisive points with your offer through the targeted use of the below options:

Thick, high quality paper

Print your offers on thicker than usual, high-quality paper. The feel of your offer is a value factor that should not be underestimated. If it fits, maybe choose one with a slightly textured finish. Discreet play with the colors of the paper is also appropriate. It doesn't always have to be white.

Order or folder

Written offers are often several pages long. Invest a little money and have professional offer folders created in your company design and, of course, make them fit the layout of your offers.

Signature

Sign the offer personally, preferably with a fountain pen with a slightly wider tip. This means no additional work for you, but it is much more valuable.

Envelopes and boxes

Like the paper, the envelopes should also look high-quality. For this, also choose paper that is a little thicker than it would normally be. If you are sending larger offers, you might even have a narrow box made for shipping.

I myself have one for sending my offers to potential lecture customers. In the case of lecture requests, I usually send books that match the offer, which can be optimally packed in my specially developed shipping box.

Postage stamps

Letters are often only provided with an inconspicuous sticker instead of a stamp. The colorful pictures on the stamps look much nicer and more valuable. So, it is better to use stamps.

As far as I know, there are even ways to have your own stamps created. That is, admittedly, a lot of effort, but if you use a lot of stamps it's a very nice idea.

Side dishes

What can you add to your offers that fit thematically and enhance the package? Depending on the industry and company, this could be:

- a detailed product description
- a product or material sample
- an image brochure
- a collection of customer testimonials
- a book - most readers will not, yet, have their own, but a book that fits your offer is highly

recommended and increases the perception of your competence enormously.

Shipping via postal service

If you cannot deliver and present your offer yourself, send it by post. The additional time it takes to send the mail is not a disadvantage in most cases.

All of the options provided to make your offer appear more professional and valuable are not that important individually. Overall, however, they have an impact that can make all the difference between an order and a rejection.

Stand out

In the case of particularly large or important offers, where the competition is perhaps also very professional and strong, it can make sense to try a little more, or perhaps significantly more than usual with the written offer. After all, you want to attract attention and stand out among the competition.

Opportunities for this are, above all:

- the presentation of your offer
- the packaging of your offer.

But what possibilities can you explore here? Basically, it's about going beyond the boundaries of what your customers expect. In addition to the variants mentioned at the beginning, there are many more different things you can do when presenting your offer.

The following ideas for multimedia support of your written offers are especially suitable for all those offers that you send by email. As discussed, sending emails is the weakest way of delivering your offers for various reasons. Support in this area is therefore very useful.

Offer strategy #41 - Include an audio file with the offer

If you do not have a chance to explain the offer to your customer in person or by telephone because there is not enough time or they do not want to, you can still speak to them. For example, you can easily record an audio file on your smartphone in which you leave your message for the customer and send it with the offer. This should still be feasible in view of the file size.

In this message you can introduce yourself, explain your offer, and provide additional information. In this way you can add a personal touch to your offer, and you will definitely stand out from the abundance of competitor material. In all likelihood, you will be the only one who addresses the customer with a spoken message.

Offer strategy #42 - Package your message as a video

It is a little more complex, but definitely more effective, to package your message to the customer in a video. Nowadays, this can also be done quickly and easily with any commercially available smartphone and a little effort.

It's not about perfection at all. Of course, the sound and picture quality must be such that your message is clearly understandable. In addition, it makes your presentation pleasant if it is good, but technically not perfect. Nobody expects a Hollywood-style film cut. Anyway, everyone will be amazed that you have also chosen this medium.

Variant 1

One variant is to simply speak your message i.e. self-introduction, information about the offer etc. into the camera.

Variant 2

If you want to present the offer yourself, you can start by speaking a sequence into the camera, as in variant 1. Then, place the offer in front of you, or place your laptop or tablet in front of you, so that the viewer can see the offer clearly. Carry out an offer presentation as if you were actually sitting across from the customer.

The only thing missing is the interaction with the customer. He or she might ask questions or raise objections at a personal offer discussion. You can do this yourself in your video. True to the motto, "At this point I am often asked by customers ..."

This variant of creating a video can also be done with little effort. Pay particular attention to the visibility, any reflections, and the image quality when filming the screen with your smartphone. The font size is also important. For this type of presentation, the font probably has to be larger than the normal, written offer, depending on how you position the camera.

A somewhat antiquated, but not at all impractical, method for this purpose is to work with a so-called table flipchart. This is a kind of ring binder in A4 or letter landscape format that you can set up on a table and then turn the pages of sheet by sheet.

Variant 3

A third, more professional way to pack your offer presentation in a video is to do it with a tool that allows your presentation to be seen on the screen. You go through this step by step and you can be filmed in a smaller window as a presenter, if you prefer.

Your laptop's built-in camera is useful for this.

Tools that are well suited for this are:

- Screenflow
  http://www.telestream.net/screenflow/overview.htm or

- Camtasia
  https://www.techsmith.de/camtasia.html but also

- Zoom https://zoom.us/ a video conference and webinar tool can be used for these purposes.

Especially if you plan to create such videos more often, the purchase of one or the other tool quickly pays for itself.

Attention data volume

If you use one of the video variants for your offer presentation, the file will very quickly become too large to be sent by email. Depending on the customer, you often no longer have a chance of delivery at 10 or 20 MB.

If so, try another way to transfer the video to be certain. Either send it by Wetransfer (https://wetransfer.com/) instead of by email, or upload your file to YouTube or Vimeo, making it not visible to the public, and just send your customer a link to view the video.

Offer Strategy #43 - Make your own website for your offer

Presenting your offer in this way is a lot more time-consuming, but you can create your own offer website, as a subpage of your website, especially for one customer.

This particularly makes sense if the project or the customer is very important to you or, if successful, a very large order beckons.

On such a website, which can only be accessed with a code that you send to the customer, you can then combine all media:

- text with a personal address to the customer
- a video which can start running automatically as soon as the website is accessed in which you greet the customer and present the offer
- the offer itself as a PDF for download
- an audio file.

You probably have more ideas of what you could put on one page. There are hardly any limits to your creativity.

While it takes more effort to create such a small promotional website, that shouldn't put you off using this strategy. If we assume that the individual components, namely the offer itself as a PDF, the accompanying letter and, if necessary, the video have to be created anyway,, such an offer website can be ready in 30 minutes with a little know-how.

In general, from my experience, this variant can be implemented very easily and unbureaucratically in small companies; in large companies and corporations the bureaucratic and technical hurdles would probably be too high.

Get noticed offline

Not only do you have creative opportunities to attract attention with your offer online, but also offline, in the real, physical world.

Offer Strategy #44 - Deliver "Shock and Awe" packages

"Shock and Awe" are exactly the states in which you want to put your customers with this type of offer packaging. The strategy is to put together a physical offer package that literally "knocks the customer's socks off."

This can concern the contents of the package or the type of delivery, or of course both combined. These "Shock and Awe" packages can also cost a lot of money, maybe a few $10s or $100s per package; certainly significantly more than a letter with your printed offer. This strategy cannot, therefore, be used economically for mass offers.

But how can you prepare such a "Shock and Awe" package? If you think one or the other idea is exaggerated or you are even shocked by it, then it could be extreme enough for a true "Shock and Awe" package. Here are a couple of ideas:

- Have your offer delivered by someone special:

- someone in disguise (to match the product) or
- a celebrity or VIP.
- Deliver the offer by drone.
- Place the offer in a suitcase with a screen that will show your video as soon as the lid is opened.
- Deliver your offer in a completely oversized box on a pallet.

Whatever you do, everything is possible, as long as this type of packaging also fits your message, your product, and the customer.

From the examples, you can already see that there are industries and products or services in which this type of supply packaging is easier to imagine and others where it might be better not to do it.

Wherever creativity is required from you, for example as an advertising agency, you could really score with such a package. If an auditor delivers their offer for the audit of a group subsidiary by drone or mounted messenger, it could very well be that they quickly eliminate themselves from the field of competitors for the contract.

Last strategy

Finally, I have one last strategy to give you. This does not actually affect the offer directly, but it is incredibly important for your success.

Bonus tip: Follow up - ALWAYS!

It is frightening how many salespeople create offers, sometimes investing a lot of time and effort, and then never contact the customer again. Mystery shopping shows time and again that there are a lot more than you would think possible.

That is also very good news for you. Your competition is potentially weak in this regard and is also among those who do not follow up on offers. This means that if you do this and stick to the customer or the offer, you will automatically be very far ahead in many industries.

Assume that your customer receives three offers, which is not that easy in some industries, and assume that these three offers are roughly comparable in terms of content, form, and price. One of the three providers follows up and keeps contacting the customer without being annoying or intrusive. The other two don't do this because they are afraid of annoying the customer and think that the customer will get in touch when he wants to buy.

In this case, which offer is the customer most likely to choose? Who has the better cards? I think you can answer this question very well yourself.

"I don't have time to follow up on all the offers," I keep hearing from sellers and entrepreneurs. If you don't have time to follow up, then the question arises as to whether you should even write an offer and invest this time beforehand.

Of course, it will not always be possible to follow up on every offer, although it should be the goal. If time is tight, then start from the top and follow up on the larger offers with priority and by phone. The smaller ones maybe only be by e-mail, which is better than not at all, and can be well standardized and possibly even automated.

"How long or how often should I follow up on my offers?" Sellers keep asking. The answer is as long or as often until the customer says YES or NO I already know that there are cases where the whole project comes to nothing. The customer does not make a decision, and, at some point, they may no longer be available. When to stop following up in these cases is a matter for you to decide.

Raise the unused potential in your offers

In summary, you have a variety of ways to turn your written offers into better dumb salespeople. If you use these, or at least some of them, consistently, you will see results.

Your offers will be noticed positively. Your customers will not dispose of these lightly. You will even get one or two words of praise for your offer from customers if you have implemented it particularly well. And—ultimately the most important thing—you will sell more and, above all, at higher prices.

Investing a little time, a lot of creativity, and a little money in your offers can bring rich rewards indeed.

I wish you every success with the implementation.

Yours,

About the Author

Foto: Matern, Wien

Marketing and price expert Roman Kmenta has been an international entrepreneur, keynote speaker, and bestselling author for more than 30 years. The business economist and serial entrepreneur makes his many years of international marketing and sales experience in the B2B and B2C sectors available to over 100 top companies as well as many small businesses and sole proprietorships in Germany, Switzerland, and Austria.

More than 25,000 people read his blog or listen to his podcast every week. With his lectures he gives salespeople, executives, and entrepreneurs food for thought on the subject of "profitable growth" and gives his listeners and readers inspiration towards a value-oriented sales and marketing approach.

www.romankmenta.com

Top strategies to enforce higher prices

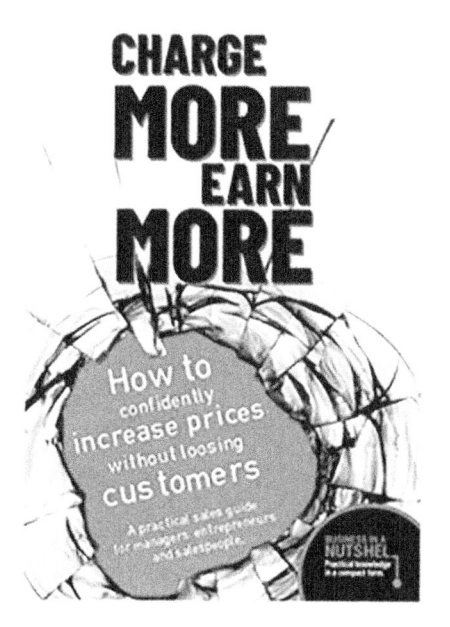

Achieving higher prices is a key success factor for most companies. A very special challenge is to carry out price increases with existing customers in such a way that the customer remains a customer. It is important to know about and implement a number of decisive strategies in sales and marketing.

This book is dedicated to these strategies. Pricing and price increases are issues that affect the entire company.

Accordingly, some of the recommended approaches are comprehensive, far-reaching, and in-depth. At the same time, you will also find tips in this book that can be implemented quickly and easily, which will make the next price increase easier and bring you a lot of money.

In this book you will learn:

- when the optimal time is for a price increase
- how not to make a price increase look like one
- how to avoid price comparability
- how to increase the value of your offer in the eyes of the customer
- how to avoid price negotiations
- which price psychological affects you should be aware of
- which arguments you can use to support a price increase
- how to raise prices without raising prices.

Higher prices, higher contribution margins, and more income. A book that pays off.

Find your USP and become unique!

Endless competitors and all of them offer the same thing, at least from the point of view of many customers.

Positioning, differentiating yourself, being unique are becoming increasingly significant for many companies. Essential for survival. It is important to find unique selling points, ideally a USP, a unique value proposition.

In this book you will get:

- A tried and tested strategy on how to find your market positioning and USP
- Ideas on how to unmistakably present your customer benefits
- Tips on how to shine through uniqueness and clearly stand out from the mediocre

- Strategies used by top brands to create differentiators
- Over 500 specific USP examples that set you apart from your competition

To be better than the competition is good. But the best strategy for higher sales, fees, and income is to be different. Best of all, unique.

Order here >>

Amazon.com - https://amzn.to/2FP4Ijg

Amazon.co.uk - https://amzn.to/33VqQ3h

Amazon.com.au - https://amzn.to/3mNZzso

Amazon.ca - https://amzn.to/2G2pknK

"In this book you will not only find generally valid explanations about USPs, but also numerous practical examples that can be adapted immediately for your particular business case. The book is not only aimed at pure USP rookies, but also at those who have already started to think about it and are looking for further inspiration. Although I haven't been dealing with USP only since yesterday, I still received valuable suggestions. Highly recommended."

Leopold Pokorny, ECDL project manager

www.elege.online / www.mentor.at

As Amazon partner I earn commission on qualified sales.

Never speechless anymore in price talks

Too expensive! Do you hear that again and again in price negotiations? You will find 118 answers to price objections in this book so that you are never speechless again in price discussions and will always have the right answer ready for handling objections. The spectrum goes from cheeky to convincing, from sensible and calculated to humorous, but always profitable!

With this book you will:

- Always find the right answer to objections in price negotiations
- Get to know new negotiation techniques and methods of handling objections
- Learn to use psychological tips and strategies effectively in price negotiations

- Make your negotiations more successful
- Get better results when negotiating prices
- Have more fun negotiating prices

Reader votes

"From pragmatic to emotional, cheeky and, above all, implementable for a wide variety of industries and situations."

"Sales are often about reframing and eloquence. You can tell that the long list has arisen from a wealth of experience that is second to none."

"Top! - I have already attended many expensive seminars and received far fewer sayings that can be used in practice."

"Cheeky, innovatively, bravely, and confidently sell your value!"

"Seldom laughed so much and found so much again!"

Order here >>

Amazon.com - https://amzn.to/3j2oeqS
Amazon.co.uk - https://amzn.to/34182zU
Amazon.com.au - https://amzn.to/2RWnibo
Amazon.ca - https://amzn.to/363IKU8

As an Amazon partner I earn commission on qualifying sales.

Printed in Great Britain
by Amazon